IMAGES OF REDEMPTION

GOD'S UNFOLDING PLAN THROUGH THE BIBLE

12 Studies for Individuals or Groups

RUTH E. VAN REKEN

SHAW

IMAGES OF REDEMPTION
A SHAW BOOK
PUBLISHED BY WATERBROOK PRESS
5446 North Academy Boulevard, Suite 200
Colorado Springs, CO 80918
A division of Random House, Inc.

Unless otherwise indicated, all Scripture quotations are taken from the *Holy Bible: New International Version* ® *NIV* ® Copyright © 1973, 1978, 1984 by International Bible Society. Used by permission of Zondervan Publishing House. All rights reserved.

Special thanks to editor Mary Horner Collins for her significant work in shaping this and countless other Bible studies into usable form. Truly we are members one of another.

ISBN: 9780877887294

Printed in the United States of America

146502721

CONTENTS

INTRODUCTION

The Bible, from beginning to end, shows us that God has a wonderful plan for his creation. When Adam and Eve sinned in the Garden of Eden, it seemed that his plan was ruined. Yet in that moment God began revealing his on-going design to redeem humanity's lost purity.

What does it mean to *redeem* something? When using this term about our relationship to God, it's easy to make it synonymous with *salvation,* i.e., the forgiveness of our sins through Jesus which makes a future life with God in heaven possible. While redemption clearly includes the concept of personal salvation, it is far more than that. The dictionary defines it thus: "to repurchase; to get or win back; to restore; to release from blame or debt; and to free from the consequences of sin." In this study we will see God's plan for future and complete redemption as well as the means and process through which he daily restores the possibility for us to live more closely to what he originally intended us to be.

But how can an infinite God communicate such a plan to finite people with finite minds? Throughout Scripture, he has done it by telling us stories. Each true story recorded there adds more shape and color to the emerging picture of how he will reclaim us and our fallen world, making us pure and perfect once more. Early sketch marks interwoven through images or symbols in the Old Testament are finally understood when fleshed out in the New Testament. But the richness and significance of details and references in the New Testament take clearest shape only when placed against the backdrop of these early pictures in the Old. As

Augustine said centuries ago, "In the Old Testament the New Testament lies hidden; in the New Testament the Old Testament stands revealed."

Take a look as God unfolds his overall plan from the first verse in Genesis to the last one in Revelation. Each study looks at a story in the Old Testament along with its fuller explanation in the New. While a short study like this can in no way do justice to the topic of redemption, we have chosen these few examples to remind us why the whole Bible is essential for our spiritual growth and encouragement. Truly, from beginning to end, God's amazing faithfulness to us and all his creation shines through.

HOW TO USE THIS STUDYGUIDE

Fisherman studyguides are based on the inductive approach to Bible study. Inductive study is discovery study; we discover what the Bible says as we ask questions about its content and search for answers. This is quite different from the process in which a teacher *tells* a group *about* the Bible, what it means, and what to do about it. In inductive study God speaks directly to each of us through his Word.

A group functions best when a leader keeps the discussion on target, but this leader is neither the teacher nor the "answer person." A leader's responsibility is to *ask*—not *tell*. The answers come from the text itself as group members examine, discuss, and think together about the passage.

There are four kinds of questions in each study. The first is an *approach question*. Used before the Bible passage is read, this question breaks the ice and helps you focus on the topic of the Bible study. It begins to reveal where thoughts and feelings need to be transformed by Scripture.

Some of the earlier questions in each study are *observation questions* designed to help you find out basic facts—who, what, where, when, and how.

When you know what the Bible says, you need to ask, *What does it mean?* These *interpretation questions* help you to discover the writer's basic message.

Application questions ask *What does it mean to me?* They challenge you to live out the Scripture's life-transforming message.

Fisherman studyguides provide spaces between questions for jotting down responses and related questions you would like to raise in the group. Each group member should have a copy of the studyguide and may take a turn in leading the group.

For consistency, Fisherman guides are written from the *New International Version.* But a group should feel free to use the NIV or any other accurate, modern translation of the Bible such as the *New Living Translation,* the *New Revised Standard Version,* the *New Jerusalem Bible,* or the *Good News Bible.* (Other paraphrases of the Bible may be referred to when additional help is needed.) Bible commentaries should not be brought to a Bible study because they tend to dampen discussion and keep people from thinking for themselves.

SUGGESTIONS FOR GROUP LEADERS

1. Read and study the Bible passage thoroughly beforehand, grasping its themes and applying its teachings for yourself. Pray that the Holy Spirit will "guide you into truth" so that your leadership will guide others.

2. If the studyguide's questions ever seem ambiguous or unnatural to you, rephrase them, feeling free to add others that seem necessary to bring out the meaning of a verse.

3. Begin (and end) the study promptly. Start by asking someone to pray for God's help. Remember, the Holy Spirit is the teacher, not you!

4. Ask for volunteers to read the passages out loud.

5. As you ask the studyguide's questions in sequence, encourage everyone to participate in the discussion. If some are silent, ask,

"What do you think, Heather?" or "Dan, what can you add to that answer?" or suggest, "Let's have an answer from someone who hasn't spoken up yet."

6. If a question comes up that you can't answer, don't be afraid to admit that you're baffled! Assign the topic as a research project for someone to report on next week.

7. Keep the discussion moving and focused. Though tangents will inevitably be introduced, you can bring the discussion back to the topic at hand. Learn to pace the discussion so that you finish a study each session you meet.

8. Don't be afraid of silences; some questions take time to answer and some people need time to gather courage to speak. If silence persists, rephrase your question, but resist the temptation to answer it yourself.

9. If someone comes up with an answer that is clearly illogical or unbiblical, ask him or her for further clarification: "What verse suggests that to you?"

10. Discourage Bible-hopping and overuse of cross-references. Learn all you can from *this* passage, along with a few important references suggested in the studyguide.

11. Some questions are marked with a ♦. This indicates that further information is available in the Leader's Notes at the back of the guide.

12. For further information on getting a new Bible study group started and keeping it functioning effectively, read Gladys Hunt's *You Can Start a Bible Study Group* and *Pilgrims in Progress: Growing through Groups* by Jim and Carol Plueddemann.

SUGGESTIONS FOR GROUP MEMBERS

1. Learn and apply the following ground rules for effective Bible study. (If new members join the group later, review these guidelines with the whole group.)

2. Remember that your goal is to learn all that you can *from the Bible passage being studied.* Let it speak for itself without using Bible commentaries or other Bible passages. There is more than enough in each assigned passage to keep your group productively occupied for one session. Sticking to the passage saves the group from insecurity and confusion.

3. Avoid the temptation to bring up those fascinating tangents that don't really grow out of the passage you are discussing. If the topic is of common interest, you can bring it up later in informal conversation following the study. Meanwhile, help each other stick to the subject!

4. Encourage each other to participate. People remember best what they discover and verbalize for themselves. Some people are naturally shier than others, or they may be afraid of making a mistake. If your discussion is free and friendly and you show real interest in what other group members think and feel, they will be more likely to speak up. Remember, the more people involved in a discussion, the richer it will be.

5. Guard yourself from answering too many questions or talking too much. Give others a chance to express themselves. If you are one who participates easily, discipline yourself by counting to ten before you open your mouth!

6. Make personal, honest applications and commit yourself to letting God's Word change you.

CREATION
God Reveals His Intentions

Genesis 1:24-31; 2:4-9, 15-25; Revelation 21:1-5, 22-27; 22:1-5

A few years ago we lived in Kenya and had several opportunities to take safaris in the wild game parks there. Though I'm not usually much of a nature-lover, these trips filled me with awe as I saw firsthand the absolute wonder of God's creative nature and power. How could he have made such a seemingly unending variety of animals, where even the stripe pattern on every zebra is unique? How did he design every species to blend so perfectly into its particular environment? What kind of God would create sunrises and sunsets that fill the skies with breathtaking colors and movement?

Truly, these safaris left me with a new sense of worship for a most worthy God. Yet they revealed only a fraction of what God did when he created the world, and they were only teasers of what is yet to come. To understand why there had to be a plan for redemption, we need to first look at what God's intention for his creation was—and still is.

1. What is your vision of a perfect world?

Read Genesis 1:24-31.

2. We see that God is the instigator and designer of the entire creative process of this world and all that is in it. What is God's assesment of his work? Why?

3. According to this passage, what is different about God's creation of humans from that of the animals? What do you think that means?

How does this difference relate to the specific role he assigned to humans (verses 28-30)?

◆ **4.** What are people and animals allowed to eat (verses 29-30)? Why only this?

What does (or doesn't) this tell you about God's original plan for his creation?

Read Genesis 2:4-9, 15-25.

5. How would you describe the world God designed for Adam and Eve?

Why do you think the man and woman could be naked and unashamed (verse 25)?

6. Which two trees are specifically named (verse 9)? What are God's instructions regarding one of them (verses 15-17)?

◆ **7.** Why do you think God gives this command about the tree? Why not simply remove it from the Garden?

Read Revelation 21:1-5, 22-27; 22:1-5.

♦ **8.** How does this picture of God's future grand finale—
the "new earth"—compare with his first creation in the
Garden of Eden (see Genesis 2:15-25)? Discuss as
many differences and similarities as you can.

Similarities		Differences	
Old	*New*	*Old*	*New*

9. What particular things make this re-creation of the
new heaven and the new earth so perfect?

♦ **10.** What do these pictures of the first creation and ultimate new creation teach you about God and his plans
for this world and those in it?

11. Second Corinthians 5:17 tells us that "if anyone is in Christ, he is a new creation; the old has gone, the new has come!" Are you a new creation in Christ? If so, in what ways have you seen God's renewing power at work in your life?

12. How would you describe the process of God's redemption in our lives? Ask God to continue giving you a clearer picture of himself as the God who loves his creation and wants to redeem it back, as well as a deepening understanding of what that means in *your* life today.

THE FIRST AND LAST ADAM
God Rescues Sinners

Genesis 3:1-12, 21-24; Romans 5:12-21;
1 Corinthians 15:45-49

How often I wish my world more closely resembled my mental picture of the original Garden of Eden—no awareness of evil, no frantic schedule to keep, no bad moods, no friction in any relationship. But my world doesn't look like that, and neither does yours. Instead of virtue, we see vice. Instead of calmness, we have chaos. Instead of gladness, we know grief. Instead of harmony, we experience hostility.

Why couldn't the world stay the way God made it? How can it ever be fixed? This study will help us to answer these questions as we look at the first Adam and the "last Adam."

1. Have you had an experience when one seemingly small mistake you made spoiled an otherwise perfect plan? How did it feel? What did you do?

Read Genesis 3:1-7.

♦ **2.** Who do you think the serpent is? What are its tactics in tempting Eve? Why do you think they work?

♦ **3.** What happens when Adam and Eve eat the fruit (see also Genesis 2:25)? Why?

Read Genesis 3:8-12, 21-24.

4. What happens when God comes on the scene? Can you relate to Adam and Eve's response in this situation? Explain.

♦ **5.** Compare the way Adam and Eve try to fix things in verse 7 with what God did in verse 21. What's the difference between the two?

6. Why would a merciful, loving God drive Adam and Eve from their perfect Garden (verse 22)?

What might have happened if they had stayed? Why would that have been a problem?

Read Romans 5:12-21.

7. We are told that through one man sin and death entered the world. How do you define *sin?* Is it different from just a mistake or error in judgment? Explain.

8. Compare and contrast what this passage tells us about Adam and Jesus.

How do their actions affect forever the rest of humankind?

♦ **9.** Why is it possible for the last Adam, Jesus, to redeem what the first Adam did? How does he do it?

Why is he the *last* Adam, when there are many people who have been and will be born after him?

10. Look for the repeated words *gift* and *grace* used throughout these verses. How would you define these two words?

From this passage, what is the gift? What is the grace? What is (or isn't) our part in the process of God's dispensing them to us?

Read 1 Corinthians 15:45-49.

♦ **11.** Compare and contrast what this passage says about the first Adam and the last. What further light do these verses shed on Adam and Jesus?

12. What do we learn about ourselves from these verses?

13. As you've studied this lesson, what truth has stood out most to you? Take time to listen and respond to anything further God may want to show you from these Scriptures.

THE FLOOD
God Judges Evil

Genesis 6:1–7:1, 11-23; 8:15-22; Matthew 24:1-14, 29-51

Daily news reports of tragedy and death can easily lead us to despair. The world seems to have gone so wrong and to be so far from what God intended that it seems impossible to believe we can ever find our way back. The message the angels sang of "Peace on earth and goodwill toward men" rings hollow. We are tempted to wonder if even God can fix it all.

One thing we often overlook when thinking about God's redemptive work is that somewhere along the way there is always a time of judgment—when evil is destroyed, good is preserved, and a fresh cycle begins that moves us closer to God's original intentions. Let's look at how God has dealt with great evil before, giving us a sneak preview of a time still to come.

1. Can you imagine a world so terrible that it would have to be destroyed? What would it look like?

Read Genesis 6:1–7:1.

*If possible, skim through all of Genesis 6–9 before
starting this lesson. It will add more understanding to
what Jesus says later on.*

◆ **2.** In our first study we read that "God saw all that he
had made and it was very good" (Genesis 1:31). How
does he feel about his creation now? What has made
the difference (6:1-6)?

3. What does God, the Creator, decide to do to his creation (6:7, 13, 17)?

4. Genesis 6:8 begins with "But," a word of contrast.
How is Noah different from other people of his day?

How does God's plan for Noah differ from his plan for
the rest of the world? Why?

Read Genesis 7:11-23; 8:15-22.

5. Compare what happens to Noah and his family with what happens to the rest of the population. What makes the difference? What is Noah's response?

Have you ever felt spared or rescued by God? What was your response?

Read Matthew 24:1-14.

6. What does Jesus say the world will be like before he returns?

In what ways does this description remind you of Noah and his day?

Read Matthew 24:29-51.

7. What does Jesus say will happen to the world he has just described (verses 29-35)?

8. How does Jesus himself directly compare this to the time of Noah (verses 36-41)? What do you believe is his point in making this comparison?

9. What is Christ's personal challenge to those who are listening to him (verses 42-47)? How do those same words challenge you?

10. What is Christ's warning to his listeners (verses 48-51)? How is that a warning to us today?

11. As you read these Scriptures, do they lead you to hope or despair? Explain.

12. Does the fact that Christ has promised to return one day and deal with evil make much practical difference to you in your everyday life? Why or why not?

13. Ask God to remind you each day of his ultimate plan and how it can help you put today's problems into better perspective. Spend time reflecting on how perfectly in control God is this very day.

THE SIGN OF THE COVENANT
God Identifies His People

Genesis 17:1-14; Galatians 3:6-8; Colossians
2:6-15; Hebrews 8:7-13

On August 26, 1967, I began a covenantal relationship with David
Van Reken. That was the day we solemnly vowed before God and
friends that, until the day one of us died, I would be his wife and
he would be my husband—no matter what. We exchanged rings
as a permanent sign and seal of our covenant together. Since then,
no matter how good or bad any particular day may be, our relationship has been based on those vows given and received. Because we know our marriage is permanent, there is deep security
to develop and grow within that relationship.

God, too, makes covenantal, redemptive promises with us. He
often gives a sign to remind us of those eternal promises. After
the flood, God gave the rainbow as a reminder of his pledge to
never destroy the world again through a flood. Today we read
about a physical and then spiritual sign that marks his relational
covenant with his people.

1. What signs or symbols are used today to mark particular agreements? Why do we need them?

Read Genesis 17:1-14.

♦ **2.** Throughout these verses, what two words does God use to describe this covenant? Why are they significant?

3. What specific promises does God make to Abraham?

What is Abraham's part in this covenantal relationship?

4. Would it be possible for a covenantal relationship like this to be broken? Why or why not?

5. What is the sign of God's covenant with Abraham?

Why do you think God chose such a mark as an appropriate reminder of this particular covenant?

6. What will happen to those who refuse this mark? Why?

Read Galatians 3:6-8.

7. What new light does this passage shed on the covenant God made with Abraham centuries before?

8. What does it mean to be "children of Abraham" in this context?

Would you consider yourself to be one?

Read Colossians 2:6-15.

9. What does Paul exhort believers to do and not do (verses 6-8)?

◆ **10.** How does he use an Old Testament sign and give it new meaning?

What does Paul's analogy here mean for you now as you seek to walk with Christ?

Read Hebrews 8:7-13.

◆ **11.** What are the basic differences between the old covenant and the new one?

12. Looking back through all the passages, compare and contrast the ways the sign of circumcision is used in the Old and New Testaments.

Old Testament	New Testament

13. Is there some place in your life where you have been doubting whether God will keep his word to you? In what ways does this study encourage you?

14. Spend some time thanking God that he is a covenantal God who keeps his promises throughout the generations. And then listen. Perhaps there is something else he would like you to consider from these Scriptures today.

THE PASSOVER LAMB

God Makes a Way Out

Exodus 11:1-8; 12:1-32; Mark 14:12-26; Romans 6:15-23

Ever have a time when, no matter how much you pray, nothing seems to change? At times it can feel that God's promises are meant for everyone but us. The Israelites certainly must have known such feelings. For centuries, ever since the days of Abraham, they had heard of a land God promised to give them. Yet, in spite of that promise, they became slaves in Egypt and remained in that condition for many generations. How could they ever be free?

Because God's ways are not our ways, he often asks us to trust him simply because he has made us a promise—not because we can understand how he plans to keep his word. Just when the Israelites thought that God had completely abandoned them, he was preparing to do one of his greatest redemptive acts in history. He provided a way for them to be delivered from death and set free from slavery; a way only God himself could provide. In so doing, he also foreshadowed a clear picture of the way he would later provide for all to escape eternal death and be set free from a different kind of slavery.

1. If you were one of the Israelite slaves in Egypt, what would be difficult about believing a promise of freedom?

Read Exodus 11:1-8.

2. Nine plagues have already been sent on the land of Egypt. What is the last plague God will send? Why is he sending it?

Read Exodus 12:1-32.

3. Describe the type of lamb that God requires the Israelites to use (verses 1-5).

Why do you think this is the only kind he will accept?

♦ **4.** What are the people to do with the lamb (verses 6-11)? Why is the blood so significant in these instructions (verses 12-13, 21-23).

5. What will happen to those who follow these instructions? What, by implication, will happen to those who do not?

Read Mark 14:12-26.

♦ **6.** What from the Old Testament story above is retained here in this New Testament story?

What is different or new?

♦ **7.** How does Jesus begin to explain the hitherto hidden meaning of the Passover Feast to his disciples (verses 22-24)?

8. Note when Jesus' meal with his disciples takes place. (Scan Mark 14–15 for events before and after). Why do you think this time of the Passover was God's appointed time for Jesus to die?

♦ **9.** In John 1:29, John the Baptist declares about Jesus, "Look, the Lamb of God, who takes away the sin of the world." How does the story of the Passover lamb in Exodus 12 shed light on the significance of Jesus as the Lamb of God?

Read Romans 6:15-23.

10. How does Paul define what a slave is in this passage (verse 16)?

11. List the positive and negative benefits of the two types of slaves he mentions (verses 19-22).

What makes the difference between which kind of slave we are?

12. We've observed the kind of slavery the Israelites endured and how God delivered them. How does the fact that Jesus is the Lamb of God relate to this matter of our slavery to sin?

13. Take time to remember all that it cost Jesus to be the Lamb of God for you. Think about the benefits you have reaped because of his sacrifice for you. For further reflection, meditate on John 18–19:37.

THE FIRE AND CLOUD
God Leads His People

Exodus 13:17–14:31; Psalm 23; Galatians 5:16-26

Some of life's hardest moments have happened when I follow what seems to be God's clear leading and wind up in a mess. I wonder: Did I hear God right? Did I make a mistake and take a wrong turn somewhere? Has he abandoned me? Why did I ever leave the safety of my previous situation and risk following God into this new place? Those are the times I wish I could *see* him with my physical eyes so everything would be plain.

The irony we find in Scripture is that even when people had the clear, tangible leading of God, sometimes they still wound up in messes and continued to complain and question. While one part of redemption involves our marvelous deliverance from sin and death, as we saw in the last study, we must not forget that redemption also includes following God over the long haul. Watch as God leads the children of Israel directly to a major obstacle in their march to freedom and see what he teaches them through it.

1. Have you, or someone you know, ever faced a situation of danger where you couldn't rescue yourself and could only wait to see what would happen? Explain the circumstances and how you felt at that moment.

Read Exodus 13:17–14:31 for the overall story.

♦ **2.** Why does God choose this particular route out of Egypt for the children of Israel (13:17-18)?

What does this tell you about God?

3. In what tangible way is God present with the children of Israel as they go through the wilderness (13:20-22)? Why is this vital for the Israelites?

Do you ever wish God would come and lead you in a similar fashion? Explain.

4. Who makes Pharaoh chase the Israelites, and to what end (14:1-4)?

Why is this important for us to know and remember?

5. What does the Israelites' reaction to Pharoah's coming reveal about them, especially after just experiencing God's miraculous deliverance from Egypt (14:10-12)?

Have you ever responded in a similar way when caught in a tough situation? Explain.

6. How does Moses respond to the people (verses 13-14)? Why does he see things differently from most of the others?

Have you ever responded *this* way when facing great difficulty? What happened?

7. When you look at this whole story of deliverance, what do you learn about God? What do you learn about those who follow him?

Read Psalm 23.

8. This psalm uses the metaphor of a shepherd to describe God. What are some of the great variety of places he leads us, his sheep?

With which of these places do you most identify at this time in your life?

9. Why could the psalmist be confident, no matter what the circumstances were?

What is the end result of the entire journey?

Read Galatians 5:16-26.

♦ **10.** Why do we no longer need a cloud and fiery pillar to lead us through life?

How are we told to live? Why?

11. Often we try to control our sin nature by pure will-power. What does Paul say is the secret to living in victory over sin (verses 18, 25)?

What does that mean to you?

12. Are you facing a figurative Red Sea experience? Whatever your circumstances, remember that God has not forgotten where you are or what you are struggling with. Take time to bring these situations to him. Ask God to give direction, hope, comfort, healing, or whatever you need. Listen to his response. He will choose how and when, but he promises to be with you and to lead you. Read Proverbs 3:5-6 for more encouragement.

MANNA
God Feeds His People

Exodus 16; John 6:25-51; 1 Corinthians 11:23-26

Throughout Scripture the children of Israel represent the story of our own struggles to follow God in true faith. For them, as for us sometimes, it seemed that no matter how faithful God had been, a new test brought back the old doubts and despair.

After the Israelites had crossed the Red Sea and moved into the wilderness, they faced what appeared to be certain starvation. With no permanent home, they could plant no crops. With no local stores, they could buy no food. How would they survive? Rather than remember what God had already done for them, they began to grumble and complain once more at his leading. Through their story we learn not only of God's limitless ability to provide for physical needs, but of his plan to provide for spiritual needs as well.

1. What types of things do you find it easy to gripe and grumble about?

Read Exodus 16:1-12.

2. When the Israelites grumble at Moses and Aaron, Moses tells them they are actually grumbling against God (verse 8). Why?

What does this teach you about human nature?

3. How does God respond to their grumbling?

What does that say to you about the character and nature of God?

Read Exodus 16:13-36.

4. What happened when the Israelites obeyed God's rules regarding the manna, and what happened when they didn't (verses 19-30)? Why?

5. Why do you think some of them disobeyed God's instructions?

6. Note how long the daily provision of manna lasted (verse 35). What does this fact tell you about God and his relationship to the Israelites?

How does this truth encourage you?

Read John 6:25-51.

7. This passage follows the story of Jesus' miraculous feeding of five thousand people (6:1-14), and he uses that event to set the scene for his claims. How does Jesus clarify what the people *want* and what they *need?*

8. Compare and contrast Jesus' claims about himself with the manna in the wilderness (verses 49-51).

♦ **9.** What are Jesus' promises for those who "eat of this bread"?

How do we eat this living bread from heaven?

Read 1 Corinthians 11:23-26.

10. What further ramifications of Jesus as the Bread of Life are explained here?

11. What is the purpose of communion according to Jesus? How does "remembering" feed our souls?

12. In what ways are you like the grumbling Israelites? How can you encourage one another not to forget God's faithfulness when you face new or difficult situations?

13. What does it mean to you that Jesus is the Bread of Life? Take time to be with him, asking Jesus to be your sustenance in ways you've never known before. Remember that he himself is the one who invites you to partake—and he has promised never to drive you away (John 6:35-37).

WATER FROM THE ROCK
God Gives Living Water

Exodus 17:1-7; John 4:4-15; 7:37-39; 1 Corinthians 10:1-4

Where I grew up, the daily temperature averaged 110 degrees in the shade. The heat that made water so essential for us to drink also dried up wells, river beds, and streams anytime there wasn't sufficient rain. At critical times, water became a carefully rationed commodity. Without it we knew we would die.

Throughout their journey in the wilderness, finding enough water to sustain life remained a chronic challenge for the children of Israel. God used this need not only to teach them more about himself, but also to continue revealing spiritual truth to us all.

1. Think of a time when you were "dying of thirst." What did it feel like? What did you do?

Read Exodus 17:1-7.

♦ **2.** The Israelites now have daily bread, but they are out of water. How is their reaction similar to or different from how they reacted before when they were hungry (see Exodus 16:1-3)?

3. How does Moses respond? How does God respond this time? Does either response surprise you?

Read John 4:4-15.

4. Describe the situation. What does the fact that Jesus is thirsty tell you about him?

♦ **5.** Why is the woman surprised by Jesus' actions (verse 9)?

6. How does Jesus compare the water from the well with what he offered (verses 10, 13-14)?

7. What is the woman's response to Jesus' offer of living water? Why?

Read John 7:37-39.

Refer to this passage and the preceding one for the next two questions.

8. How does Jesus further explain the meaning of living water in this passage? How are we to receive it?

Why do you think he calls this "living" water?

9. What specific promises does Jesus make to all who will drink of this living water?

Read 1 Corinthians 10:1-4.

♦ **10.** How does Paul tie together the story we read in Exodus and the picture of Christ as the giver of living water?

11. Read together Psalm 63:1. David writes, "O God, you are my God, earnestly I seek you; my soul thirsts for you, my body longs for you, in a dry and weary land where there is no water." How would you rate your spiritual thirst today?

12. Spend time reflecting on Jesus' promise to fill you with springs of living water. What is your part? What is his part? Let the Holy Spirit lead you now in whatever else you need to think or pray about.

THE TEN COMMANDMENTS
God Gives Laws for Life

Exodus 19:1-8; Deuteronomy 5:1-22; Romans 7:14–8:8

For some, the fact that God has given us the Ten Commandments makes him seem like a frowning traffic cop with hand held high, preventing us from going where we want to go, or a judge who sentences us with awful finality for the wrongs we have done. Many prefer not to consider the existence of a God who makes up such seemingly obstructionistic rules. So why did God give these commandments in the first place? How do they apply to our lives today?

God's plan of redemption continues to unfold as Jesus reveals more fully what the law is about and how it points to a far greater law—the grace-filled law of the Spirit of life.

1. How did you respond to rules as a child?

Read Exodus 19:1-8.

2. Where are the Israelites now? What does God pledge to them? On what condition?

♦ **3.** In light of God's covenant, what is the purpose of the law they are about to receive?

Read Deuteronomy 5:1-22.

♦ **4.** Why do you think God reminds the Israelites of his past dealings with them (verse 6; Exodus 19:4)?

♦ **5.** In verses 1-5, Moses reminds them of the covenant we have just discussed. How does God identify himself (verse 6)?

Why is this an important preface to what he is about to say?

6. In the first four commandments, what is the basic relationship God is dealing with?

How would you sum up this group of commandments?

♦ **7.** What is the basic relationship God is dealing with in the last six commandments?

How might our world be different if each of us followed these?

8. Do you think these commandments were encouraging or discouraging for the Israelites to hear? Explain.

What is your response as you have read them? Why?

Read Romans 7:14–8:8.

9. What does Paul say is the basic problem when he tries to keep the law (7:14-23)? Would more knowledge correct the problem? Why or why not?

10. What is the solution to Paul's dilemma (8:1-4)?

What makes this solution effective when nothing seemed to help before? (Discuss not only the facts of these first verses, but also what they can mean in your everyday life.)

11. Compare and contrast the two types of minds in 8:5-8. How does each relate to keeping God's law?

At this point in your life, which of these two minds describes you? Explain.

♦ **12.** See John 1:15-18. In light of Paul's discussion above, what's the difference between what has come to us through Moses and what has come to us through Jesus?

13. How is living by the Spirit different from living under the law? Ask God to show you more and more what that means. Also, ask him to reveal any areas where you may still be trying to walk according to your own understanding and human efforts rather than trusting him in all things.

THE BRONZE SERPENT
God Offers Salvation

Numbers 21:1-9; John 3:5-18

People used to call me "Miss Question Box" when I was a child. I wondered and worried about everything, including what could really happen "if I just believed." Every Christmas I would try to believe enough to acquire the most desired toy for that year. But what happened if a piece of doubt slipped in during the repeated mantras of what I was trying to believe? Did I have to start all over again? How much belief—and in what—did I need to get God to do what I wanted him to do?

Unfortunately, my childish misperceptions about what it means to believe are all too often present in us as adult Christians. We can easily have faith in our "faith"—in what we believe *about* God—rather than having a deeply rooted faith *in* God himself. Once more, by looking at the Israelites' story we catch a glimpse of God's plan and of what it means to respond to God *in* faith rather than trying to control him *by* faith.

1. Is believing different from having faith in something? Why or why not?

Read Numbers 21:1-9.

◆ **2.** At this point in Israel's desert wanderings they are encountering other nations. What do you learn about war in ancient times?

Why do they completely destroy everything?

3. Contrast the Israelites' attitudes in verses 1-3 and 4-5. Why the difference?

4. What is God's reaction to all their griping (verse 6)?

Thinking back to the Garden of Eden, what might be the significance of the means God uses to get his message across in this situation?

5. How do the people and Moses respond to God's action against them (verse 7)?

6. What is God's answer this time (verse 8)? Why the difference in his two reactions to them?

7. Until God's intervention, all the Israelites were under the sentence of death. What is ironic about the symbol God uses as a means of their salvation?

What is God's part in this process? What is the Israelites' part?

8. Imagine yourself in this situation with the Israelites. How do you think you would have felt when Moses told you God's solution for the crisis? Would you have obeyed? Why or why not?

Read John 3:5-18.

9. What do you learn about the person with whom Jesus is talking, and what is the gist of their conversation?

10. How many times does the phrase "believes in him" occur (verses 14-18)? To whom does the "him" refer?

In this context, what does it mean to *believe?*

11. Compare what Jesus says about himself and spiritual salvation to what Moses told the Israelites about physical salvation. What things are similar? What are different? What is God's part? What is our part?

12. Which promise of God seems more remarkable to you—his promise to the children of Israel in the Numbers passage, or his promise to Nicodemus (and us) in John 3:16? Which is harder to believe? Why?

13. Are there areas in your life which seem as hopeless as what the Israelites faced in the wilderness? How can looking to Jesus, your Savior, make a difference in those places? Do you really believe *in* him, or simply *about* him? Spend time meditating on these questions and ask God to show you his answers.

THE HIGH PRIEST
God Provides a Mediator

Leviticus 16; Hebrews 9:1-15; 7:22-28; 4:14-16

We have looked at several stories through the Bible that have helped explain God's process of redemption in our lives. These stories are rich with meaning—tangible pictures God has given us to explain intangible realities. And there is no greater need for the help of a tangible image than when it comes to understanding how sinful human beings can have a relationship with a holy God.

John 14:6 tells us that Jesus is the truth, the life, and the only way we can ever come to God the Father. How do we understand that awesome truth? Why do we need this go-between? Today's study reveals the amazing images God has given us to understand Jesus' role as our priest and sacrifice.

1. What is the value of having a mediator settle a dispute between two parties?

Read Leviticus 16:1-34.

♦ **2.** What facts do you learn about Aaron and about the tabernacle in verses 1-2?

What does God *forbid* Aaron to do? Why?

♦ **3.** In verses 3-5, what does God tell Aaron *to* do?

What do you think is the significance of such elaborate ritual?

4. Identify the types of sacrifices Aaron is to offer (verses 3-5), who each one is for, and why each one is needed (verses 11, 15, 20-22, 24-25).

♦ **5.** All these rituals are part of the "Day of Atonement." What is *atonement* (verse 30)?

6. Per God's instructions, how often are these rituals to be performed?

Who alone can offer the sacrifices? Why not every person for him or herself?

Read Hebrews 9:1-15.

7. Using this passage along with what you have just learned from Leviticus 16, compare the Old Testament means for atonement with that presented in the New Testament.

	Old	*New*
The tabernacle (vss. 1-6; 11)		
Who offered sacrifices and for whom (vss 7, 11-14)		
Requirement for priest to enter (vss. 7, 12)		
Kind of sacrifice required (vss. 7, 12-13, see 26-28)		
Results of sacrifice (vss. 9, 13-15)		

Read Hebrews 7:22-28.

8. In what ways is Jesus different from the high priests of the old covenant?

9. How does this make him a "guarantee of a better convenant"?

Read Hebrews 4:14-16.

10. What is Jesus able to do as our mediator and high priest? Why?

11. Because we have a great high priest now in heaven, what are we able to do? Why?

12. When you consider what it means to have Jesus, God's Son, as your high priest, and the sacrifice he made to pay the price of atonement for your sins, what is your response? Take a few moments to ponder the wonder of these things. Express your response to God in whatever way you find most meaningful.

THE TEMPLE
God Dwells with His People

1 Kings 8:1-30; Matthew 27:45-54; 1 Corinthians
3:16-17; 6:12-20

After their long journey through the wilderness, the Israelites
finally settled in the promised land of Canaan. The temporary
tabernacle tent they carried on their journey was eventually re-
placed with a beautiful temple built by King Solomon. The finest
materials and the overlay of gold and fine jewels made it a place
that truly reflected God's glory, a fitting place for God to dwell
among his people.

For one last time, we look at both the foreshadowing and the full
completion of God's redemptive work in our lives through the
image of his glorious temple. Our study begins when Solomon's
temple is completed and the people prepare for its dedication.

1. If God is everywhere, why do we need places like
temples, churches, and synagogues?

Read 1 Kings 8:1-21.

♦ **2.** What did Solomon do before bringing the ark of the covenant to the new temple?

Why was it such a big deal to get the ark there?

♦ **3.** When the ark arrived at the temple, where was it placed? Why?

4. What happened after the ark was placed in the temple (verses 10-11)? Why?

How do you think you would have felt if you had been one of the priests?

Read 1 Kings 8:22-30.

5. In verses 14-21, King Solomon recounts the history of this temple for the gathered crowd. What do you learn about God through Solomon's prayer? About David? About Solomon's character?

6. Solomon begins his dedicatory prayer with praise. What are some of the things Solomon praises God for?

From what you know of the Israelites, what are some things you would add to this list if you were Solomon?

7. How does Solomon answer the question, "Can God dwell on earth?" (verses 27-28)?

Read Matthew 27:45-54.

8. This is the ending of the story of Jesus' crucifixion. What significant thing happened at the temple when Jesus died?

What did this mean for the Jews then? For us now? (See Hebrews 4:14-16 for further reference.)

Read 1 Corinthians 3:16-17.

9. What is the temple Paul speaks of here?

How is it the same as Solomon's temple? How is it different?

10. How valuable is this new temple? Why do you think God seems to care for it so much?

Read 1 Corinthians 6:12-20.

♦ 11. We live in a day when sexual sin is rampant, much like it was in the days of the Corinthians. It's easy to begin excusing it as something "everyone does." What does this passage say about such an idea?

12. Why do you think Paul makes such a point that our bodies and not just our souls are important?

What does he stress as the reason we should not give our bodies over to sin?

13. What does it mean for you today that your body is a temple of the Holy Spirit?

14. Take some time to reflect on what God has taught you in this study of redemption stories through the Bible. What new things have you discovered? For what are you thankful?

LEADER'S NOTES

Question 4. Without sin, there would be no death—for animals or human beings. Romans 8:18-25 tells us that all of creation now waits for God to restore it to its original state.

Question 7. The knowledge of evil itself is soul-contaminating. As persons made in his image, however, we must have the ability for true choice—even the choice to obey or disobey God.

Question 8. Among other differences and similarities, ask the group the significance of the fact that while the tree of life remains, the tree of the knowledge of good and evil is gone. One thought might be that in this new creation, there is full protection from all evil—both the practice and perhaps even the knowledge of it.

Question 10. God is good and what he has done and will do is good and perfect. Evil and its effects around us aren't God's original or ultimate plan for his creation. They are the work of Satan, the father of lies, the destroyer. When we look at the beginning and end of creation, we see God's true heart for us and his world.

■ Study 2/The First and Last Adam

Question 2. In Revelation 12:9, we're told that the serpent who appeared to Adam and Eve is the devil, or Satan.

Question 3. For the first time Adam and Eve see themselves as they really are—naked and exposed, not only physically but also spiritually. They have, in fact, acquired the knowledge of good and evil that they had desired. At this moment, they began a course toward physical death (Genesis 2:17), and spiritual death occurred as well. Until the Holy Spirit gives new life, we also are spiritually dead in our sins (see Romans 5:12; 6:23). This is why we need a second birth (see Ephesians 1:1-10; John 3:1-18).

Question 5. For the first time in history, humans try to cover the effects of their sin. When God comes, however, no amount of fresh leaves can hide their nakedness. In his mercy God makes a better covering, but it costs the life of an animal. Physical and spiritual death have come to God's creation because of sin.

Question 9. Through the first Adam we have physical life, sin, and death. Through the second Adam, Jesus, we have spiritual life, forgiveness, and eternal life. That is possible only because of Jesus' sinlessness. Because he had no sin, he had no judgment of death against him as we do; thus his death could pay the price for what we owe. This is why he is the only way to the Father (John 14:6).

Question 11. These are the only two men in the history of the world who began life in a sinless state—Adam, because he was created that way, and Jesus, because he was God. For additional study, read Luke 4:1-13, comparing the temptation experiences of the first and last Adams.

■ Study 3/The Flood

Question 2. The positive identification of the Nephilim and why they are called "sons of God" remains a mystery. Some believe they were fallen angels; others say maybe they were a godly line of Seth's descendents, or even ungodly kings of that day. They were apparently giants. Interestingly, later the children of Israel were afraid to enter the promised land because there were "Nephilim" there (see Numbers 13:31-33).

■ Study 4/The Sign of the Covenant

Question 2. When God repeatedly says, "My covenant," he is backing up his promise with his very character. Throughout the Bible, God makes many covenants with people. In all cases God is the initiator. Some covenants, as with Noah, are totally one way; God simply states what he will do no matter what. Other covenants, such as this one with Abraham, involve a certain response or accountability from the other party. In the end, God will always fulfill his promises because, even when we are faithless, "he will remain faithful, for he cannot disown himself" (2 Timothy 2:13).

Question 10. It's interesting to note that this analogy was also used by the prophet Ezekiel, when he talked of foreigners with "uncircumcised hearts" desecrating the temple (see Ezekiel 44:7-8).

Question 11. The author of Hebrews is quoting the prophet Jeremiah, who foretells a new spiritual covenant with God. As Paul relates in Colossians 2, this has been brought to fruition in Christ.

■ Study 5/The Passover Lamb

Question 4. Hebrews 9:22 says "without the shedding of blood there is no forgiveness" (see also Leviticus 17:11). From the beginning God told Adam and Eve that the price of sin was death. Something or someone had to die for that price to be paid. When blood is poured out, it is a sign that this condition for the forgiveness of sins has been met.

Question 6. The Feast of Unleavened Bread is another name for the Passover Feast, which was instituted by God in Exodus 12 when he delivered the Israelites from Egypt. The religious Jews of Jesus' day were still observing this centuries-old feast, remembering the night the angel of death "passed over" their houses because the blood of the sacrificed lamb was on their doorposts.

Question 7. Knowing of his impending death and resurrection, Jesus fills this Passover meal, often called the Last Supper, with new meaning. Here Jesus institutes the "Lord's Supper," or Communion, as a permanent reminder of the blood he shed and death he suffered in our place. Each time we take the wine and bread, we are to remember the price it cost him to be our Savior. See also 1 Corinthians 11:23-26.

Question 9. Referring back to Exodus 12, have the group come up with as many similarities between the Passover lamb and Jesus as they can. For example, the only way the eldest born of any family in Egypt could escape death on the night of the original Passover was for an unblemished lamb to die in his place / Christ was sinless; the lamb's blood had to be brushed over the doorposts / we must be "under" Christ's blood to be saved; God accepted the lamb's sacrifice / God accepts Jesus' death as a substitute for our own, etc. For more on Jesus as the Lamb of God, see also Revelation 1:5; 5:6-14; 7:9-10, 14-17; 12:11; and 13:8.

■ Study 6/The Fire and Cloud

Question 2. Though at times God's leading may not make sense to us, he leads us knowing full well how good his ultimate plan is. He remembers that we are dust (Psalm 103:14) and promises that he will never test us beyond what we can endure (1 Corinthians 10:13).

Question 10. In John 14:15-18, Jesus tells his disciples (and us) that through the Holy Spirit, he will continue to be with them as their shepherd and guide, even after his physical departure from them.

■ Study 7/Manna

Question 9. In the mystery of the new birth, we initially "eat" of Christ when we trust in his death as the substitution and payment for our own sin and well-deserved spiritual death. Somehow, as we do that, the Spirit of God enters us and gives us spiritual birth—a birth into eternal life (see John 3). But it is more than just a birth. We must grow. Abiding in Christ and eating this "bread of life" also involves a decision to trust God for each day's needs, each day's worries, each day's tasks. It involves prayer, meditating on his Word, and seeing more of who God is. Somehow, as we feed on the bread of life in these ways, we are spiritually nourished in the same mysterious way that literal bread nourishes our physical body.

■ Study 8/Water from the Rock

Question 2. Read Numbers 20:1-13 for a comparison story of this event.

Question 5. The Samaritans and the Jews held each other in mutual contempt. While both had monotheistic theologies, the religious and political differences between them caused such hatred that a Jew could be considered ceremonially unclean if he or she had any contact with a Samaritan. The fact that a Jewish man would not only approach but ask a favor from a Samaritan woman—particularly one of such ill-repute—would have been shocking in Jesus' day.

Question 10. Paul explains here how both the bread and the water God gave the Israelites during their days in the wilderness are what Bible scholars call *typologies:* symbols in the Old Testament of something fulfilled in the New.

It's interesting to note that Jesus is the rock from which the water is poured. He is not the water itself. Even this simple detail fits in with what Jesus said—that the water he will *give* is the Holy Spirit. This is not the same "I Am" declaration as when he talked about *being* the bread of life.

◼ Study 9/The Ten Commandments

Question 3. Without the law, we could not understand how to obey God, for we would not know his standards or expectations. See Romans 7:7-12 for more on this.

Question 4. Obedience is based on trust, hence God's reminder that they could trust him.

Question 5. God's name, *Yahweh,* ("Jehovah" or "LORD") was considered by the Jewish people to be the most holy name of God; too holy even to be spoken out loud. "In particular, Yahweh was the God of the Patriarchs. . . . Yahweh . . . is the name of a Person, though that person is divine. . . . It brings Him into relationship with other, human, personalities. It brings God near to man" *(The New Bible Dictionary,* p. 478. Eerdmans, Grand Rapids, Mich.: 1962).

Question 7. See Mark 12:28-34 for Jesus' summation of the law.

Question 12. Often, in spite of believing that our salvation is a gift—not something we can earn—we turn Jesus' principles for living an abundant life into deadening rules. But in Christ we can live freely through his grace and love.

■ Study 10/The Bronze Serpent

Question 2. The Hebrew term for *destroy* in Numbers 21:2 refers to the "irrevocable giving over of things or persons to the LORD, often by totally destroying them" *(Life Application Bible,* p. 250. Tyndale House, Wheaton, Ill., 1988). See also Numbers 33:50-56, where God gives the Israelites a clear command that, when they go to war in the new territory he is giving them, they are to destroy everything. God did not want syncretism with foreign gods or his people mixing with pagan tribes.

■ Study 11/The High Priest

Question 2. Aaron was Moses' older brother, his spokesman and his right-hand man throughout the wanderings in the wilderness. Exodus 39–40 relates God's instructions for Aaron's high-priestly role. Aaron's sons were anointed as priests with him, but were later destroyed by fire when they didn't follow God's commands (Leviticus 10:1-3).

To get a better picture of the tabernacle, God's dwelling place among the Israelites, see Exodus 39:32–40:38 for a summary of the layout. You may want to show your group a picture of a picuture of the tabernacle for reference.

Question 3. Because high priests were also sinners, they had to first prepare and cleanse themselves. This included offering a sacrifice for their own sin before they could ask forgiveness for the sins of the people. We must never forget that God is holy and cannot look at sin. Sometimes our "easy access" to God through Jesus makes us forget that.

Question 5. *Atonement* is more than just trying to make up for mistakes we've made. It means "to make full reparations for an offense or injury." As sinners, there's nothing we can do to turn aside God's holy and righteous anger at our sin, and there's nothing we can do to make full reparation. In fact, Romans 6:23 tells us that the "wages of sin is death." Death is God's just judgment for sin, and it must be carried out. But how?

God, in his mercy, provides a way of atonement under the old covenant through the substitutionary death of an animal. He also gives a graphic picture of his love through the image of the *scapegoat*—he not only forgives our sins but removes them far away from us. This foreshadows the coming role of Jesus as *both* our intercessory high priest and our actual sacrifice for sin.

Because Jesus has both cleansed us from our sins and paid the penalty for them, we can now have peace with God. That is true atonement—the reconciliation of humankind to God through Christ our mediator.

▦ Study 12/The Temple

Question 2. See Exodus 25:10-22 for God's instructions about the ark of the covenant. It served as a symbol of the divine guidance the Israelites knew as they moved from slavery to freedom and of God's presence among them.

Question 3. When God gave instructions for the tabernacle in the wilderness (a prototype of the temple), he told them to make a curtain to set apart a section called the "holy of holies." This was the place they were to keep the ark of the covenant. As Solomon constructs the temple, he designs that same inner sanctuary.

This holy area was divided from the rest of the temple by a heavy curtain or veil. No ordinary person could ever enter. Only the high priest could enter once a year to plead with God on behalf of the people and only after offering sacrifices for his own sin. To break that law meant death. This gives us another picture of how, without Christ, we are completely unable to come to the Father on our own. His holiness and our sin cannot meet without Jesus' sacrifice making atonement for our sin.

Question 11. A particular heresy of that time (and perhaps now?) was that you could not sin with your body as long as your spirit or soul was "pure." Paul says such a dichotomous view is wrong. Our very bodies are the place where God resides. They are the means through which we express the reality of the life within us—for good or for evil.

WHAT SHOULD WE STUDY NEXT?

To help your group answer that question, we've listed the Fisherman Guides by category so you can choose your next study.

TOPICAL STUDIES

Angels, Wright

Becoming Women of Purpose, Barton

Building Your House on the Lord, Brestin

The Creative Heart of God, Goring

Discipleship, Reapsome

Doing Justice, Showing Mercy, Wright

Encouraging Others, Johnson

The End Times, Rusten

Examining the Claims of Jesus, Brestin

Friendship, Brestin

The Fruit of the Spirit, Briscoe

Great Doctrines of the Bible, Board

Great Passages of the Bible, Plueddemann

Great Prayers of the Bible, Plueddemann

Growing Through Life's Challenges, Reapsome

Guidance & God's Will, Stark

Heart Renewal, Goring

Higher Ground, Brestin

Integrity, Engstrom & Larson

Lifestyle Priorities, White

Marriage, Stevens

Miracles, Castleman

One Body, One Spirit, Larson

The Parables of Jesus, Hunt

Prayer, Jones

The Prophets, Wright

Proverbs & Parables, Brestin

Satisfying Work, Stevens & Schoberg

Senior Saints, Reapsome

Sermon on the Mount, Hunt

A Spiritual Legacy, Christensen

Spiritual Warfare, Moreau

The Ten Commandments, Briscoe

Who Is God? Seemuth

Who Is Jesus? Van Reken

Who Is the Holy Spirit? Knuckles & Van Reken

Wisdom for Today's Woman: Insights from Esther, Smith

Witnesses to All the World, Plueddemann

Worship, Sibley

BIBLE BOOK STUDIES

Genesis, Fromer & Keyes
Exodus, Larsen
Job, Klug
Psalms, Klug
Proverbs: Wisdom That Works,
  Wright
Jeremiah, Reapsome
Jonah, Habakkuk, & Malachi,
  Fromer & Keyes
Matthew, Sibley
Mark, Christensen
Luke, Keyes
John: Living Word, Kuniholm
Acts 1-12, Christensen
Paul (Acts 13-28), Christiansen
**Romans: The Christian
  Story,** Reapsome
1 Corinthians, Hummel

**Strengthened to Serve
  (2 Corinthians),**
  Plueddemann
Galatians, Titus & Philemon,
  Kuniholm
Ephesians, Baylis
Philippians, Klug
Colossians, Shaw
Letters to the Thessalonians,
  Fromer & Keyes
Letters to Timothy, Fromer &
  Keyes
Hebrews, Hunt
James, Christensen
1 & 2 Peter, Jude, Brestin
**How Should a Christian Live?
  (1, 2 & 3 John),** Brestin
Revelation, Hunt

BIBLE CHARACTER STUDIES

**David: Man after God's Own
  Heart,** Castleman
Elijah, Castleman
Great People of the Bible,
  Plueddemann
**King David: Trusting God for
  a Lifetime,** Castleman
Men Like Us, Heidebrecht &
  Scheuermann

Moses, Asimakoupoulos
Paul (Acts 13-28), Christensen
Ruth & Daniel, Stokes
Women Like Us, Barton
**Women Who Achieved for
  God,** Christensen
Women Who Believed God,
  Christensen

Printed in the United States
by Baker & Taylor Publisher Services